# MYSTERIOUS MESSAGES,
# CODED CONUNDRUMS, ANONYMOUS NOTES

# EDWARD GOREY
## a book of postcards

Pomegranate

PORTLAND, OREGON

Pomegranate Communications, Inc.
19018 NE Portal Way, Portland, OR 97230
800-227-1428   pomegranate.com
sales@pomegranate.com

An **Edward Gorey**® licensed product
© 2010 The Edward Gorey Charitable Trust

Pomegranate publishes books of postcards on a wide range of subjects.
Please contact the publisher for more information.

ISBN 978-0-7649-5528-0
Item No. AA649

Cover designed by Ronni Madrid

Printed in Korea

29  28  27  26  25  24  23  22  21  20      15  14  13  12  11  10  9  8  7  6

To facilitate detachment of the postcards from this book, fold each card along its perforation line before tearing.

Much like an eccentric scientist in a gothic legend, Edward Gorey (American, 1925–2000) brought to life from the laboratory of his mind altogether new, intriguing, perplexing, often playfully sinister personalities. Ill-fated children with baleful faces; anthropomorphic creatures of untraceable biological lineage; shadowy, haunted adults, forever on the verge of mysterious errands: these are but a few of the irresistible characters who populate Gorey's world. His drawings and stories, set in a vaguely Edwardian time frame with a decidedly English overtone, have a special genius that resides in the effect of what is left unseen and unwritten. As evident in the thirty enigmatic images presented here, Gorey's illustrated texts often guide the reader to the point just before the crescendo of events and then let the imagination draw the ominous or hilarious conclusions.

Gorey's rise to popularity as master of the amusingly strange and unexpected was not immediate. He worked as a staff artist and art director at Doubleday and at the legendary Looking Glass Library at Random House. He later freelanced as a widely respected book designer. His work has been exhibited at the Galerie Keel in Zurich, Switzerland; the Institute of Contemporary Art in Boston; and Lincoln Center Library, Graham Gallery, and Gotham Book Mart Gallery in New York City, among other venues.

Gorey's enormous talent extended to theater as well. The designs for his Broadway revival of *Dracula* were nominated for two Tony Awards and won Best Costume Design, and he has received acclaim for his work both on and off Broadway.

# EDWARD GOREY

## MYSTERIOUS MESSAGES, CRYPTIC CARDS, CODED CONUNDRUMS, ANONYMOUS NOTES

Illustration for *Mystery!*

pomegranate.com

# EDWARD GOREY

## MYSTERIOUS MESSAGES, CRYPTIC CARDS, CODED CONUNDRUMS, ANONYMOUS NOTES

Illustration from *The Willowdale Handcar*

pomegranate.com

# EDWARD GOREY

## MYSTERIOUS MESSAGES, CRYPTIC CARDS, CODED CONUNDRUMS, ANONYMOUS NOTES

Untitled drawing

# EDWARD GOREY

**MYSTERIOUS MESSAGES, CRYPTIC CARDS,
CODED CONUNDRUMS, ANONYMOUS NOTES**

Illustration from *Leaves from a Mislaid Album*

# EDWARD GOREY

## MYSTERIOUS MESSAGES, CRYPTIC CARDS, CODED CONUNDRUMS, ANONYMOUS NOTES

Illustration for *Mystery!*

pomegranate.com

# EDWARD GOREY

## MYSTERIOUS MESSAGES, CRYPTIC CARDS, CODED CONUNDRUMS, ANONYMOUS NOTES

Detail from an untitled drawing

pomegranate.com

# EDWARD GOREY

## MYSTERIOUS MESSAGES, CRYPTIC CARDS, CODED CONUNDRUMS, ANONYMOUS NOTES

Illustration for *Mystery!*

# EDWARD GOREY

## MYSTERIOUS MESSAGES, CRYPTIC CARDS, CODED CONUNDRUMS, ANONYMOUS NOTES

Untitled drawing

pomegranate.com

# EDWARD GOREY

## MYSTERIOUS MESSAGES, CRYPTIC CARDS, CODED CONUNDRUMS, ANONYMOUS NOTES

Untitled drawing

pomegranate.com

# EDWARD GOREY

## MYSTERIOUS MESSAGES, CRYPTIC CARDS, CODED CONUNDRUMS, ANONYMOUS NOTES

Detail from an untitled drawing

pomegranate.com

# EDWARD GOREY

## MYSTERIOUS MESSAGES, CRYPTIC CARDS, CODED CONUNDRUMS, ANONYMOUS NOTES

Illustration from *The Glorious Nosebleed*

pomegranate.com

# EDWARD GOREY

## MYSTERIOUS MESSAGES, CRYPTIC CARDS, CODED CONUNDRUMS, ANONYMOUS NOTES

Untitled drawing

pomegranate.com

# EDWARD GOREY

## MYSTERIOUS MESSAGES, CRYPTIC CARDS, CODED CONUNDRUMS, ANONYMOUS NOTES

Illustration from *The Awdrey-Gore Legacy*

pomegranate.com

# EDWARD GOREY

## MYSTERIOUS MESSAGES, CRYPTIC CARDS, CODED CONUNDRUMS, ANONYMOUS NOTES

Untitled drawing

pomegranate.com

# EDWARD GOREY

## MYSTERIOUS MESSAGES, CRYPTIC CARDS, CODED CONUNDRUMS, ANONYMOUS NOTES

Illustration from *The Object Lesson* (detail)

pomegranate.com

# EDWARD GOREY

## MYSTERIOUS MESSAGES, CRYPTIC CARDS,
## CODED CONUNDRUMS, ANONYMOUS NOTES

Illustration from *Cultural Slag,* by Felicia Lamport

pomegranate.com

# EDWARD GOREY

## MYSTERIOUS MESSAGES, CRYPTIC CARDS, CODED CONUNDRUMS, ANONYMOUS NOTES

Untitled drawing

pomegranate.com

# EDWARD GOREY

## MYSTERIOUS MESSAGES, CRYPTIC CARDS, CODED CONUNDRUMS, ANONYMOUS NOTES

Untitled drawing

pomegranate.com

# EDWARD GOREY

## MYSTERIOUS MESSAGES, CRYPTIC CARDS, CODED CONUNDRUMS, ANONYMOUS NOTES

Illustration from *The Remembered Visit*

pomegranate.com

# EDWARD GOREY

## MYSTERIOUS MESSAGES, CRYPTIC CARDS, CODED CONUNDRUMS, ANONYMOUS NOTES

Illustration from *The Chinese Obelisks*

# EDWARD GOREY

## MYSTERIOUS MESSAGES, CRYPTIC CARDS, CODED CONUNDRUMS, ANONYMOUS NOTES

Untitled drawing

# EDWARD GOREY

## MYSTERIOUS MESSAGES, CRYPTIC CARDS, CODED CONUNDRUMS, ANONYMOUS NOTES

Untitled drawing

pomegranate.com

# EDWARD GOREY

## MYSTERIOUS MESSAGES, CRYPTIC CARDS, CODED CONUNDRUMS, ANONYMOUS NOTES

*The Pointless Postcard*

# EDWARD GOREY

## MYSTERIOUS MESSAGES, CRYPTIC CARDS,
## CODED CONUNDRUMS, ANONYMOUS NOTES

Detail from an untitled drawing

pomegranate.com

# EDWARD GOREY

## MYSTERIOUS MESSAGES, CRYPTIC CARDS, CODED CONUNDRUMS, ANONYMOUS NOTES

Illustration for National Postcard Week, 1996

pomegranate.com

# EDWARD GOREY

## MYSTERIOUS MESSAGES, CRYPTIC CARDS, CODED CONUNDRUMS, ANONYMOUS NOTES

Untitled drawing

pomegranate.com

# EDWARD GOREY

## MYSTERIOUS MESSAGES, CRYPTIC CARDS,
## CODED CONUNDRUMS, ANONYMOUS NOTES

Illustration for *Mystery!*

pomegranate.com

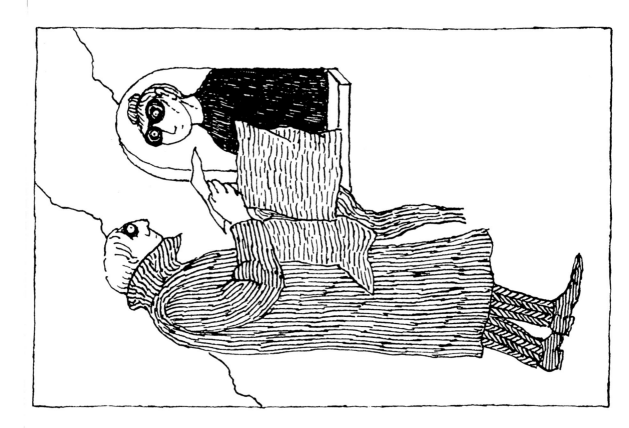

# EDWARD GOREY

## MYSTERIOUS MESSAGES, CRYPTIC CARDS, CODED CONUNDRUMS, ANONYMOUS NOTES

Illustration from *The Twelve Terrors of Christmas,*
by John Updike

pomegranate.com

# EDWARD GOREY

## MYSTERIOUS MESSAGES, CRYPTIC CARDS, CODED CONUNDRUMS, ANONYMOUS NOTES

Illustration to promote the play *The Dead of Winter*

pomegranate.com

# EDWARD GOREY

## MYSTERIOUS MESSAGES, CRYPTIC CARDS, CODED CONUNDRUMS, ANONYMOUS NOTES

Illustration from *Cultural Slag,* by Felicia Lamport

pomegranate.com